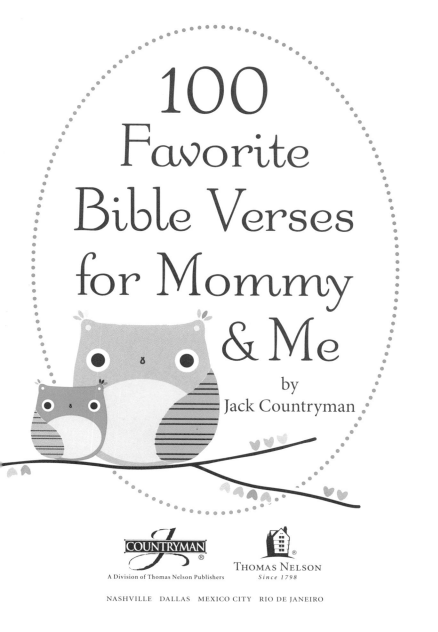

100
Favorite
Bible Verses
for Mommy
& Me

by
Jack Countryman

COUNTRYMAN ®

A Division of Thomas Nelson Publishers

THOMAS NELSON
Since 1798

NASHVILLE   DALLAS   MEXICO CITY   RIO DE JANEIRO

Published in Nashville, Tennessee, by Thomas Nelson. Thomas Nelson is a trademark of Thomas Nelson, Inc.

Thomas Nelson, Inc., titles may be purchased in bulk for educational, business, fund-raising, or sales promotional use. For information, please e-mail SpecialMarkets@ ThomasNelson.com.

ISBN-13: 978-1-4003-1814-8

Printed in China

14 15 16 17 18 DSC 7 6 5 4 3

Introduction

As a mother, you have been chosen to love, nurture, protect, and care for the precious gift of your child. The Bible is God's gift for life, and this book has been created as an encouragement for you and your little one. The topics that have been chosen will enrich your life and bring you and your child closer to your heavenly Father. As you share the Scriptures and meaningful thoughts, may they bring joy, peace, and contentment to your mind and to your heart.

Jack Countryman

Contents

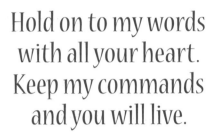

Hold on to my words
with all your heart.
Keep my commands
and you will live.

Proverbs 4:4 NCV

The Lord of Comfort

As one whom his mother comforts,
so I will comfort you.
ISAIAH 66:13

God has promised in this passage that He will comfort you. When life is wonderful and the excitement of your new child is fresh, He will celebrate with you the joy that you are experiencing. When sickness comes to your precious child, God will comfort you and guide your every step. The love that God has for you and your child is both unconditional and everlasting; therefore, embrace His love and share it with the precious gift God has given you.

The love that God has for you is never going to change.

Me

God Has Promised to Always Be with You

I will strengthen you, yes, I will help you,
I will uphold you with My righteous right hand.
ISAIAH 41:10

God's Word is strong and true. He has promised to be with you in all that you do. What you do with His promises is what matters most. Claim your position as God's child, and do not be afraid. You have the power to overcome every challenge in life when you apply His Word. He will protect you and sustain you.

What God has given, no one can take away.

Mommy

Jesus Loves Your Child

Then they brought little children to Him,
that He might touch them. . . . And He took them up
in His arms, laid His hands on them, and blessed them.
Mark 10:13, 16

You can rest assured that your child is loved beyond your imagination. Jesus cares about you and the child you have been given. Daily come to Him in prayer to seek guidance and wisdom. Let the love Jesus has for you flow through you to your child. You will be blessed, and so will your child. Someone has said, "Children are not things to be molded but people to be unfolded."

As your child depends on you,
learn to depend on your Creator.

Me

God's Love Never Changes

The LORD will perfect that which concerns me;
Your mercy, O LORD, endures forever;
Do not forsake the works of Your hands.
PSALM 138:8

The one thing that is certain and will never change is that God loves you with an everlasting love. Speak to Him daily, share His precious Word, and pray daily for His divine guidance. God will come to you when you humbly seek Him, because He has promised to be with you always. His Spirit will help you.

God's gifts put your best dreams to shame.

Mommy

The Lord Will Not Forget You

Can a woman forget her nursing child,
and not have compassion on the son of her womb?
Surely they may forget, yet I will not forget you.
ISAIAH 49:15

God has sealed you in His heart. You have been chosen by Him to be His daughter. The love that He has for you is the very love He wishes for you to have for your child. It is never changing, unconditional, and everlasting. Take time each day to thank God for His eternal love, and let your heart overflow with His love to the one you have been given to cherish.

Love your child as God loves you.

You Are Precious

Since you were precious in My sight,
you have been honored, and I have loved you.
Isaiah 43:4

Because God created you in His image, you are precious to Him. Because God created you for His glory, He wants the world to see some of His majesty and goodness through you, and He wants to crown you with His own splendor. He has not promised to keep you out of the wilderness or away from the desert, but if you belong to Him, He does promise to sustain you and renew your life when times are difficult.

You can always count on God.

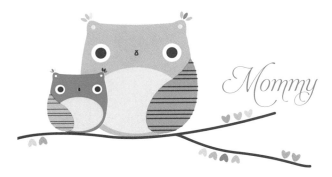

Mommy

We All Need a Shepherd

For the Lamb who is in the midst of the throne will shepherd them and lead them to living fountains of waters. And God will wipe away every tear from their eyes.
REVELATION 7:17

Sometimes it may be hard for you to accept the fact that you need a shepherd. You may think you can manage your life without the help of anyone. It is true that God has given you the ability to think for yourself and know what is right and wrong. But you will find that when you wander through life on your own, your selfish desires lead you into pitfalls. You can rest assured that God waits patiently to comfort you and wipe away your tears.

Let God handle your sorrow and tears.

Me

God Will Take Care of You

I will sing to the LORD,
Because He has dealt bountifully with me.
PSALM 13:6

Jesus loves you and promises to be with you from the very moment you were born. Everything about you is very special to God, and He wants you to grow and become someone who will reflect who He is and bring Him glory. Since the Lord is righteous, He wants you to grow and act in a righteous way. Through His Spirit, He will give you exactly what you need.

God is ever by your side.

Mommy

God's Reward

> *Behold, children are a heritage from the LORD,*
> *The fruit of the womb is a reward.*
> PSALM 127:3

In ancient times, having many children was regarded as a symbol of strength. This was particularly true in an agricultural economy, since the helpful hands of children increased productivity. In today's culture electronic technology is prominent. Guard carefully the things you wish your children to learn and become involved with. The care and training you give them will reflect on the adults they become.

Cover your children with love; they are your heritage.

God's Commitment Is Everlasting

I have loved you with an everlasting love.
JEREMIAH 31:3

God's love is so wonderful because it is everlasting. From the very first moment you were conceived, you were loved; when your mother carried you in her womb, you were loved. When you were born and you entered into the world, you were loved. As you grow and begin to talk, you will be loved. God has pledged His love to you. He walks with you in every circumstance. He has finished your portrait. Through Christ, you can and will be successful.

God's love is unconditional.

A Mother's Blessing

*Blessed is she who believed, for there will be a fulfillment
of those things which were told her from the Lord.*
Luke 1:45

Mary was blessed because she accepted by faith that she was to be the mother of Jesus. The child that has been given by God to you will fill your life with wonder, happiness, challenges, and a certain sense of accomplishment. As you raise and nurture your child, seek God's guidance. He will give you His wisdom and help you in countless ways. May you be filled with blessings that come from being a mother.

Blessings are a gift; cherish each one.

Me

You Are a Blessing

I will cause showers to come down in their season; there shall be showers of blessing.
Ezekiel 34:26

You are a blessing to those who love you and want the very best for you. Enjoy the precious moments of your childhood, because these memories will seem to fade as you grow older.

♥ ♥ ♥ ♥

Your early years are to be remembered, recorded, and enjoyed.

Mommy

God Is with You

*My Presence will go with you,
and I will give you rest.*
EXODUS 33:14

God desires to be ever present in your life as a mother. He only asks for an invitation to be included in everything you do. When decisions are to be made about your child, He wants to be included. When your family has a crisis, He wants to be included. Your life will be filled with many choices; let His presence guide you, and may you find rest in the One who loves you.

God will always be with you.

Me

God Lives in You

I will dwell in them and walk among them.
I will be their God, and they shall be My people.
2 CORINTHIANS 6:16

When Jesus comes into your heart, He lives there through the Holy Spirit. You need to know how important it is to have a personal relationship with God and what it means to live each day with Jesus in your heart.

♥ ♥ ♥ ♥

God has promised to live with you and walk with you.

Mommy

A Mother's Delight

> *Delight yourself also in the LORD,*
> *And He shall give you the desires of your heart.*
> **PSALM 37:4**

When you choose to walk with God every day, you become His delight. He takes pleasure in placing His love and joy within your heart. As you fulfill the many responsibilities of motherhood, He wants you to spend time living in His unconditional love. Be content with what you have and who you are. Let the love you have for Jesus be contagious to your child.

God delights in blessing you.

Me

You Can Always Come to God

You are my hiding place.
PSALM 32:7

You can come to God for safety and comfort. God's goodness is waiting for you. Let each step you take be filled with His guidance and love. You have been created for a special purpose. May each day bring you closer to the One who has given you life. He has promised to bless you when you trust Him with all your heart.

Jesus is waiting for you.

Mommy

God Wants to Be Included

In all your ways acknowledge Him,
And He shall direct your paths.
PROVERBS 3:6

God's guidance is more than sufficient for the tests and trials you will face as a mother. God has blessed you by giving you the gift of a child. Include Him in all you do; look expectantly for Him to direct your path. Do not hesitate to ask God for the little things that would help you become the mother He wishes for you to be.

Let God have His perfect way, and you will be blessed.

Me

A Lesson for Every Child

The fear of man brings a snare,
But whoever trusts in the LORD shall be safe.

PROVERBS 29:25

One of the hardest lessons you will need to learn is how and when to trust in the Lord. This is one of God's greatest desires for you. When you walk with God and learn to trust Him, He will bless you beyond all that you can imagine and give you all the confidence you will ever need.

God-given wisdom begins with trust.

Mommy

The Lord Is Your Best Teacher

Take firm hold of instruction, do not let go;
Keep her, for she is your life.
PROVERBS 4:13

The Lord is your Teacher, Friend, Adviser, and the One who cares for you more than anyone else ever could. He has promised to never leave you nor forsake you. Seek His help often; turn to Him when being a mother becomes a great challenge. Let Him give you the peace that only God can give. He will bless you with His presence and show you how precious you are in His sight.

Knowledge, wisdom, and understanding
of God are your keys to life.

Me

God Is the Great Comforter

You, LORD, have helped me and comforted me.
PSALM 86:17

God has promised to be your Comforter. He will lift you up. He is there to listen and to comfort you. He is the One who will stick closer than a brother. Come to God, and He will give you all the comfort you will ever need.

God is waiting just for you.

Take the First Step

Draw near to God and He will draw near to you.
James 4:8

God will always give you all the space you want. He has never been known to be an intruder in anyone's life. He gives you an invitation to draw near to Him. When you choose to do that, everything in life changes. God has promised to give you the peace that passes all understanding. Let each day be filled with His presence.

He is waiting just for you.

Me

God Is Your Best Cheerleader

May He grant you according to your heart's desire,
And fulfill all your purpose.
We will rejoice in your salvation,
And in the name of our God we will set up our banners!
PSALM 20:4–5

God has one great desire for you, and that is for you to succeed in everything you choose to do. You have been created for a special purpose. He will love you with a love that outlasts all human love. He has promised a love that will endure every test and a love that will be loyal to you through a lifetime of success and failure.

♥♥♥♥

You can count on God in every way.

Mommy

Godly Exercise Has Many Benefits

*For bodily exercise profits a little, but godliness
is profitable for all things, having promise of
the life that now is and of that which is to come.*
1 TIMOTHY 4:8

It has been said that bodily exercise strengthens your heart and improves your health. When you spend time with God each day, He will strengthen your spiritual heart and give you the confidence to live in His presence. You only need to let go and allow God to be the essential part of your life. When you do this, you will experience all the joys of motherhood, and your relationship with God will have a richer, fuller meaning.

A strong spiritual heart has many benefits.

Me

Your Life Should Be Filled with Love

And we have known and believed the love that God has for us. God is love, and he who abides in love abides in God, and God in him. Love has been perfected among us in this: that we may have boldness in the day of judgment.
1 JOHN 4:16–17

Yo u were created with the love of God in your heart. It is a gift that He gives everyone. Let the love you have been given shine brightly for others to see. When you let the light of God's love flow to those around you, He will bless you and give you the confidence to live each day for His glory.

There is nothing more important than God's love for you.

Mommy

Your Eyes Are the Windows to Your Soul

The light of the eyes rejoices the heart,
And a good report makes the bones healthy.
PROVERBS 15:30

What you choose to see, read, and enjoy with your eyes will become a road map to your life. Spend time enjoying the gifts that God has given you, and thank Him for His generosity. The attitude and gratitude of your life will begin to blossom. The Bible encourages you to be transformed by the renewing of your mind, that you may prove what is the good and acceptable will of God. Everything begins with what we choose to see with our eyes.

Feast your eyes on the child God has given you.

Me

God Is Constantly Watching

When you lie down, you will not be afraid . . .
For the LORD will be your confidence
PROVERBS 3:24, 26

There is a God who is watching over you; do not be afraid. His love will surround you and comfort you wherever you go and whatever you do. You are precious to God, and He always wants the very best for you. Learn early to come to Him daily; look for God's guidance and comfort, for He is your confidence.

"Little ones to Him belong. They are weak but He is strong."

Mommy

Focus on God's Love

*Now may the Lord direct your hearts into
the love of God and into the patience of Christ.*
2 THESSALONIANS 3:5

Directing your heart into the love of God will only happen when the Lord becomes your priority and you choose to spend time with Him daily. The patience of Christ is a part of growing closer to Him moment by moment. As a mother, you will face times when patience is necessary. Let the love of Jesus fill your heart as you walk closely with Him.

Spiritual growth happens when you meditate on God's love.

Me

Nothing Can Separate You from God

*For I am persuaded that neither death nor life, nor
angels nor principalities nor powers, nor things present
nor things to come, nor height nor depth, nor any other
created thing, shall be able to separate us from the
love of God which is in Christ Jesus our Lord.*
ROMANS 8:38–39

You have been created in God's image, and from the
beginning He has set His love on you. When we accept His love through faith in Jesus, nothing can ever
break the bonds of love that He creates, and no one is
able to snatch us out of our Father's hands. If God, the
uncreated One, is for us, then nothing can separate us
from the One who created us.

Our security in Him is absolute.

Mommy

Everything Begins with Jesus

"For the Father Himself loves you, because you have loved Me, and have believed that I came forth from God."
JOHN 16:27

When you consider your journey as a Christian mother, it is essential to recognize that the love of God has been given to you because of the great sacrifice of Jesus. He stands in the gap as your Intercessor before God. He brings your praises, adorations, requests, and need for guidance to your heavenly Father, who wants to be in the center of your life. Praise Him daily for His generous gift.

The love of God is unconditional.

Me

Jesus Christ Is Your Model

Therefore be imitators of God as dear children.
EPHESIANS 5:1

As a child of God, you are called to be more like Him. The thoughts you think and the words you speak should show the person you are becoming in your Christian walk. When you speak kind words, you will encourage others. Seek God's blessing, and the love of God will flow through you.

As a child of God, be like your heavenly Father.

Mommy

God Is Just a Prayer Away

Do not worry about anything, but pray and ask God for
everything you need, always giving thanks.
PHILIPPIANS 4:6 NCV

As a mother, there will be certain times when circumstances will cause you to worry. The Bible clearly invites you to pray about whatever may concern you and ask God for everything you need. God desires to bless you and fill your life with His presence. Worry creates a vacuum that only God can fill. Let each day be filled with the joy of coming to the throne of grace through prayer.

Giving thanks is one of the keys to a deeper walk with God.

Me

God Hears Your Prayers

The LORD is near to all who call upon Him,
To all who call upon Him in truth.
PSALM 145:18

Prayers that you learn early in life are like seeds planted in the ground. Every time you pray, spiritual water helps you grow and develop into the child God intends you to be. Let the daily habit of coming to God in prayer be one of the first things you learn. You will be blessed, and your heavenly Father will be glorified.

God is patiently waiting to hear your prayer.

Mommy

God Is Always for You

For I know the thoughts that I think toward you,
says the LORD, thoughts of peace and not of evil,
to give you a future and a hope.
JEREMIAH 29:11

As a mother, you are very special to God. He desires for you to walk closely with Him. He cares about you today and every day in your future. Invite Him into your world, and enjoy the blessings that only He can create. When God is part of your daily life, the peace that passes all understanding will be with you.

You are precious in His sight.

Me

The Lord Is Faithful

The Lord will keep all His promises;
he is loyal to all he has made.
Psalm 145:13 NCV

All that God has made bears the marks of His hand. You, my precious one, are a part of His marvelous creation. You can count on His mercy and love in all that you do. With each step you take and each word you speak, He will be with you. Learn early in your life the message of His grace and forgiveness. He is the One who loves you with an everlasting love.

Everything the Lord does is right.

Mommy

God Never Sleeps

The LORD shall preserve your going out and your coming in
From this time forth, and even forevermore.
PSALM 121:8

Sometimes it is very hard to realize and accept that the Lord is ever present. You become so wrapped up in your little world that you neglect to invite Him into every area of your life. God always wants the very best for you, both as a person and as a mother. Spend time with Him, sharing your hopes, dreams, and innermost thoughts. When you do, you will experience the joy only He can give.

Trust in the Lord with all your heart.

Me

Depend on His Word

He also taught me, and said to me:
"Let your heart retain my words;
Keep my commands, and live."
PROVERBS 4:4

God's Word has been written just for you. It is what you do with it that matters most. You are God's child, and He has given you the power to live for Him when you apply His Word to your life. God invites you to be strong in the Lord and to look to Him every day.

Hold on to His Word with all your heart.

Mommy

God Has Wisdom for You

For the Lord gives wisdom;
From His mouth come knowledge and understanding;
He stores up sound wisdom for the upright;
He is a shield to those who walk uprightly.
PROVERBS 2:6–7

God has promised to give wisdom to those who ask. When you love God and seek His wisdom, He will make it available to you. He is waiting with open arms for you to ask, so He can grant you the understanding you need as a mother. So ask, and He will give you wisdom that is "better than rubies" (Proverbs 8:11).

Wisdom is yours for the asking.

Me

Pleasing God Is a Learned Process

*Walk as children of light . . . finding out
what is acceptable to the Lord.*
EPHESIANS 5:8, 10

As you grow, you will naturally learn many things. What you say and do is important to who you will become. Your thoughts and words should bring honor and glory to God. He intends for His children to become beacons of light to show the way to spiritual safety for others.

A shining light brings hope.

Mommy

The Lord Has Broad Shoulders

Cast your burden on the LORD, and He shall sustain you;
He shall never permit the righteous to be moved.
PSALM 55:22

When you give God any burden that you carry, you open yourself to the leading and guidance of the Holy Spirit. God has never wanted you to carry your burdens alone. He cares about every situation. Being a mother is a blessing, but it can also be challenging. Let God be in the center of everything you do.

Build your life on God's righteousness.

Me

God's Protection

*Behold, I am with you and will
keep you wherever you go.*
Genesis 28:15

God has promised to be with you to guide your steps
and keep you safe. As you grow, learn to look to Him
in all that you do. His love will surround you, protect
you, and give you all the reassurance you will ever need.
You belong to God, and He belongs to you.

*There is someone who is closer than you
can imagine. Rest in His presence.*

Mommy

Abide in God's Presence

I will say of the LORD,
"He is my refuge and my fortress;
My God, in Him I will trust."
PSALM 91:2

God wants your relationship with Him to be filled with joy and gladness. In Him you have a Protector who loves you with an everlasting love. When being a mother becomes difficult, you can always turn to your heavenly Father. You can place any problem in His love and guidance.

The Lord is your security, and in Him you can find rest.

Me

Trust Is an Absolute

Trust in the LORD with all your heart,
And lean not on your own understanding.
PROVERBS 3:5

When you learn to trust in the Lord with all your heart, the foundation for your Christian life will be established. God will place within your heart a sense of what is right and wrong. His guidance is more than sufficient for all the tests and trials you will face. Therefore, open your heart and let the One who loves you with an everlasting love provide you with His wisdom.

Dependence on God is much like leaning
on a giant oak tree. It will never fall down!

Mommy

A Mother's Reward

Indeed we count them blessed who endure.
JAMES 5:11

As your child grows, your life as a mother changes. You have the responsibility over every aspect of your child's life. With His Spirit leading you, you will endure, your child will be blessed, and your reward will be the result of your time and attention. Rejoice in the opportunities that God has given you as a mother.

A mother is blessed when she endures.

Me

You Were Born to Be Blessed

The mouth of the righteous is a well of life.
PROVERBS 10:11

God's Word will sustain you throughout all of your life. He will protect you and give you everything you need. Learn, grow, and be a blessing to others. God wants to bless you so your life and words will bless others.

The words of a good person are like
pure silver. (Proverbs 10:20 NCV)

Mommy

Everything Comes from God

The Lord is my light and my salvation; whom shall I fear?
The Lord is the strength of my life.
PSALM 27:1

When you discover that everything in life that has importance comes from God, you will be given the wisdom you need to fulfill your responsibilities. The patience to overcome the challenges you encounter come from allowing God to be part of your everyday life. Depend on His Spirit to help you be the mother He wants you to be.

Jesus is the light.

God Gives Us All Things to Enjoy

God wants everyone to eat and drink and be happy in his work. These are gifts from God.
ECCLESIASTES 3:13 ICB

God desires that your life be filled with joy and happiness. From the moment you are born, His love surrounds you. Whatever talents you may have are gifts from God; therefore, let His light shine through you. Learn early to trust in Him for all things, and give Him your very best effort in all you do.

True joy comes from the living God.

You Cannot Outgive God

> *"Give, and it will be given to you: good measure,*
> *pressed down, shaken together, and running over*
> *will be put into your bosom. For with the same measure*
> *that you use, it will be measured back to you."*
> LUKE 6:38

The generosity of your heart to share God's love with others is a part of your deeper walk with God. The Lord asks you to give of your time, talent, and money to help proclaim His glory. He will guide your steps as a mother and bless all that you do for Him. God has a plan designed just for you.

When you give, you will be blessed.

Me

Giving Is a Way of Life

And remember the words of the Lord Jesus, that
He said, "It is more blessed to give than to receive."
ACTS 20:35

There is a natural instinct to selfishly look out for yourself. The words *me* and *mine* are naturally a part of everyone's vocabulary. God's way is different: when you give of your time, talent, finances, and possessions, true happiness finds you. When others are more important than yourself, life becomes meaningful. Paul, in the Bible, found his life by losing it. He lived his life by not counting it dear. When he learned to love God's will over everything else, he realized that obeying God yielded the greatest joy of life.

Be generous to others.

Mommy

Centered in Christ

Therefore, if anyone is in Christ,
he is a new creation; old things have passed away;
behold, all things have become new.
2 CORINTHIANS 5:17

As a new Christian, you leave all the old, sinful things of your past behind and go forward with a clean slate. When Jesus comes into your life, everything changes—the way you think and the choices you make. God wants your relationship with Him to become the most important part of your life.

There are many benefits when you are restored by Christ.

Me

The Holy Spirit Is Your Guide

*I will instruct you and teach you
in the way you should go;
I will guide you with My eye.*
PSALM 32:8

Listen to your parents. God is guiding you through them to help you become the person He wants you to be. God will guide you through His Spirit. You need only to ask and He will always be there. When you open your heart to your heavenly Father, He will shower you with His love.

He is with you every hour of every day.

Mommy

When God Forgives, He Forgets

I, even I, am He who blots out your transgressions for My
own sake; and I will not remember your sins.
ISAIAH 43:25

God wants you to walk faithfully with Him every day. He has chosen to blot out your transgressions and remember them no more because of His great love for you. When Jesus died on the cross and paid the ultimate sacrifice for you, your sins were forgiven, and you are white as snow in God's eyes. Thank Him often for His love and generosity. Live each day to glorify His holy name, and let the light of His countenance surround you.

Whatever has caused you to stumble, leave it behind.

Me

God's Gift for Everyone

The gift of God is eternal life in Christ Jesus our Lord.
ROMANS 6:23

From the moment you were born, God, through His love and tender mercy, has offered you a forever relationship with Him through His Son, Jesus Christ. As you grow, you can fully enjoy God's blessings by learning to live by faith and obedience. He wraps you in His loving care. His love toward you never changes. Every good thing that happens in your life is by His grace that will wash over you like sunlight on a cloudless day.

God loves you just the way you are.

Mommy

Freedom Comes from Jesus

"You shall know the truth,
and the truth shall make you free."
JOHN 8:32

When you choose to abide in God's Word, you will learn the truth of Scripture. You will receive freedom that releases you from any bondage you may have and draws you closer to your heavenly Father. When you are obedient to God's Word, you build your relationship with Him, which will protect you from the evil one and allow you to experience God's love to the fullest.

The secret to freedom is to abide in God's Word.

Me

Everything Comes from God

*Now He who establishes us with you
in Christ and has anointed us is God.*

2 CORINTHIANS 1:21

You are God's special gift. He has given His Spirit to be with you in all that you do. Seek God daily for His wisdom. As you grow in the Lord, let Him be the most important thing in your life. Let His love surround you. His mercy and grace are like new beginnings every morning.

God gives you strength.

Mommy

He Watches Over You

*For the eyes of the LORD run to and fro throughout
the whole earth, to show Himself strong
on behalf of those whose heart is loyal to Him.*
2 CHRONICLES 16:9

The Lord is on your side. He is watching over you when you choose to be loyal to Him and build a relationship with Him. Through His Spirit, He will guide you in all that you do and provide a way for you to live and serve Him with a joyful heart. These are the blessings that come to you as a mother when you walk with God daily and share your concerns, hopes, and dreams with Him.

"I will never leave you nor forsake you." (Hebrews 13:5)

Me

God Knows Everything About You

Your eyes saw my substance, being yet unformed.
And in Your book they all were written,
The days fashioned for me,
When as yet there were none of them.

PSALM 139:16

God knows everything about you, even before you were born. He loves you just the way you are. He knows your weaknesses and strengths. He knows everything you need and want. He knows what makes you smile and what makes you sad. He knows all about you because you belong to Him.

You are a child of God.

Mommy

God's Kindness Is a Gift

> *"For the mountains shall depart and the hills
> be removed, but my kindness shall not depart
> from you, nor shall my covenant of peace be
> removed," says the LORD, who has mercy on you.*
> ISAIAH 54:10

God has promised that His covenant of peace will never be removed from those who walk with Him. God's kindness is designed to give you everything you need to care for your child and share the knowledge of God's love. He desires to walk beside you, giving you comfort and strength.

What God has promised, no one can take away.

Me

You Have a Friend in Jesus

There is a friend who sticks closer than a brother.
PROVERBS 18:24

You will make friends and have people you will be close to in life. God has promised to be with you always. He will be the Friend that will always be loyal to you no matter what. Remember, He is with you wherever you go, whatever you do.

You can always count on God.

Mommy

Seek God with All Your Heart

_Then you will call upon Me and go and pray to Me, and I
will listen to you. And you will seek Me and find Me when
you search for Me with all your heart._

JEREMIAH 29:12–13

Finding God is not a monumental task, but one that
requires a commitment of your heart. God wants all
of you and waits for you to open your life to Him. As a
mother, you only have to be intentional with the priori-
ties of your life. When God is first, you will find Him
and receive the blessings He has promised.

Pray to God and He will listen.

Me

You Will Never Be Left Alone

The LORD your God is with you wherever you go.
JOSHUA 1:9

When you do God's will in God's way with God's help, no one or nothing can stand in the way. When you live in the presence of God and invite Him into every area of your life, the joy of the Lord will surround you, and you will be blessed.

♥ ♥ ♥ ♥

God is with you no matter where you go or what you do.

Mommy

Trust in God

Every word of God is pure. He is a shield
to those who put their trust in Him.
PROVERBS 30:5

Experiences in life often prevent you from trusting others; however, God can always be trusted. He has promised to love you unconditionally. He has also promised to forgive you when you disappoint Him. You need only to repent and seek forgiveness. Let His shield be your strength, and trust Him in all that you do.

Trusting God begins one step at a time.

Me

Grace Is a Gift Because of God's Goodness

To each one of us grace was given
according to the measure of Christ's gift.
EPHESIANS 4:7

By God's loving grace you are created in the image of Christ. Your life is an unfinished portrait, but God knows you perfectly and loves you completely just the way you are. You are His masterpiece—His workmanship of grace and love—His work of art. As you grow, He will continue to paint the color of your life in such a way that you will glorify Him. Though your life remains on the canvas, God has seen the finished portrait.

His eternal eyes know exactly where
you need His greatest attention.

Mommy

God's Word Lasts Forever

"Heaven and earth will pass away,
but My words will by no means pass away."
MARK 13:31

Your life will change when you accept that Jesus has all the answers. The Word of God is your pathway to happiness, peace, and contentment. The more you allow His Word to be a part of your life, the happier you will be as a person and as a mother. God's Word is like building blocks that give you protection from the storms of life. Let each day be filled with a time for meditating on His Word.

Every answer to life is found in Scripture.

God's Word Is a Road Map for Life

I love Your commandments
More than gold, yes, than fine gold!
PSALM 119:127

God's Word is a priceless treasure designed to show you His love and direction for life. When you read His Word and learn His commandments, you will build a strong foundation for your life. As you learn your way in the world, God's Word will be the compass to show you what is important and how you should live.

You never get lost when you live God's way.

Mommy

God's Guiding Spirit

*When He, the Spirit of truth, has come,
He will guide you into all truth; for He will not
speak on His own authority, but whatever He hears
He will speak; and He will tell you things to come.*

JOHN 16:13

God's Spirit lives within the heart of every Christian. He has been placed there to be your guide and provide you with His wisdom. You need only to ask for His guidance, and He will lead you to safety. The eye of the Lord is ever present, and you can rely on Him in all circumstances. Come to Him daily with an open heart, and let His Spirit fill you with the power of His presence.

Rely on God's guidance.

Me

Show and Tell God's Way

Show me Your ways, O Lord;
Teach me Your paths.

Psalm 25:4

The Lord is waiting to show you how to live, act, and be more like Him. When you come to Him in prayer, He will tell you through His Spirit the things that are pleasing to Him. The Bible says, "This is the way, walk in it" (Isaiah 30:21). Listen to what God has to say, and you will be blessed.

God is your Guide and Teacher.

Mommy

God Will Take Care of You

*My God shall supply all your need
according to His riches in glory by Christ Jesus.*
PHILIPPIANS 4:19

God has the ability to supply everything you need. His plans are for you to glorify Him and live an abundant life. God wants you to place Him first and walk with Him daily. When you are fruitful in serving Him, He blesses you, so serve Him with a pure heart.

Whatever you need, God is able to supply.

Me

God Keeps His Promises

He who promised is faithful.
HEBREWS 10:23

The one Person you can trust is God. Whatever He has promised, He will do. The Bible is filled with many promises, and all are designed to show you the way to live. Everything you need can be found in God's promises.

God's promises are true.

Mommy

Guard Your Heart

Keep your heart with all diligence,
for out of it spring the issues of life.
PROVERBS 4:23

As a mother, your emotions run very deep when it comes to your children and family. It is important to guard your heart and choose only to let things in that bring honor and glory to your heavenly Father. When you do, joy and peace will fill your life. God wants the very best for you and He will walk closely with you. Invite Him in today.

Let God fill your heart.

Me

You Are Created in God's Image

God created man in His own image; in the image of God
He created him; male and female He created them.
GENESIS 1:27

Praise God for His marvelous creation of you! You are one of a kind, conceived and woven together. You are the work of God that has been created in your mother's womb. You are truly an awesome wonder. Every part of you is a skillful demonstration of the creative power of God, who has a special plan and purpose for your life.

The Holy Spirit will guide you, protect you,
and surround you with His everlasting love.

Mommy

Wait on the Lord

Those who wait on the LORD shall renew their strength;
they shall mount up with wings like eagles, they shall
run and not be weary, they shall walk and not faint.
ISAIAH 40:31

Waiting entails confident expectation and active hope in the Lord. When you walk faithfully with the Lord, you will experience a spiritual transformation. The Lord will give endurance to those who trust Him. Mount up and spread your wings for God's glory; you will be filled with His presence, and His love will be contagious to those around you.

Let God renew you.

Me

God Is the Great Provider

The LORD is my shepherd;
I shall not want.
PSALM 23:1

When you talk to God, you will find that He is listening and will answer every one of your prayers. God wants to hear from you, and He wants you to know He cares about everything that happens to you and about you. The more you talk to Him, the better you will get to know Him. He is waiting just for you, every hour of every day.

The Good Shepherd will provide for you and protect you.

Mommy

The Gift of Peace

> *"Peace I leave with you, My peace I give to you;*
> *not as the world gives do I give to you.*
> *Let not your heart be troubled, neither let it be afraid."*
> JOHN 14:27

Jesus gives you peace. His peace banishes fear and dread from your heart, because He is in control of all your circumstances. His peace comes from a supernatural source. It keeps you from fear and worry because it brings you straight to Him. He has promised to give you the peace that passes all understanding, no matter what you are facing.

When you have worries, take them to Jesus.

Me

God's Indescribable Gift

Thanks be to God for His indescribable gift!
2 CORINTHIANS 9:15

You are the most precious gift anyone could ever want. You are a special treasure that has been created by God's design, and there is no one exactly like you. God has a plan that has been created just for you. As you grow, let His love surround you so that all that you say and do will bring honor and glory to the One who created you in His image.

God's greatest gift is Jesus.

God Works in You

> *[Be] confident of this very thing,*
> *that He who has begun a good work in you*
> *will complete it until the day of Jesus Christ.*
> PHILIPPIANS 1:6

God is always faithful to finish what He starts. The closer you walk with God and the more you allow Him to lead you as a mother, the more you will be blessed and God will be glorified. Invite Him into every area of your life, and let His light shine through you in such a way that everyone will see the love and joy of Jesus.

Whatever Jesus starts, He will finish.

Me

God's Plan for You

"Follow Me, and I will make you fishers of men."
MATTHEW 4:19

Jesus wants you to follow Him and teach others about Him. During His time on earth, Jesus was teaching, preaching, healing, and instructing people so that they might have a relationship with Him. Jesus wants you to have that same kind of relationship with Him, and to share it with others.

The choice is yours.

Mommy

Live Close to Him

He who dwells in the secret place of the Most High shall abide under the shadow of the Almighty.
<small>PSALM 91:1</small>

When you choose to live close to God, you will have security that cannot be shaken. He has promised that you shall abide in His shadow. Your walk begins with trust in the heavenly Father. He desires to walk beside you in all your circumstances. Give everything to Him.

There is safety when you abide in the presence of God.

Me

Trust and Hope Go Hand in Hand

Our heart shall rejoice in Him,
Because we have trusted in His holy name.
Let Your mercy, O LORD, be upon us,
Just as we hope in You.
PSALM 33:21–22

When you learn to trust in God with all your heart, you soon recognize that God is the One in charge and He is your only hope. When dependence on Him becomes your way of life, things that seem difficult are easier to handle because of His strength and power. Say yes to God's mercy; He knows what you need and wants you to be strong and at peace in all that you do. God stands ready to help you make the right choices. Look to Him daily to experience a deep fellowship with Him.

Put your hope and trust in God.

Mommy

Fear Not

There is no fear in love; but perfect love casts out fear . . .
[s]he who fears has not been made perfect in love.
1 JOHN 4:18

At some point in life, you will experience a certain measure of fear. And it is what you do with it that matters most. You must claim your position as God's child. You have the power to overcome fear when you apply God's Word to your life. Proclaim God's Word for every situation because you are a child of the King.

God can rescue you from all your troubles.

Me

Fear Is Not an Option

The LORD is my light and my salvation;
Whom shall I fear?
PSALM 27:1

God has promised to be your light, so you need not be afraid of the dark. He is your Protector and will always be with you. He is always there to help you make the right choices. When you lean on Him, He will always be your Guide to find all the peace and comfort you will ever need.

Perfect love casts out fear. (1 John 4:18)

Mommy

Use Kind Words

Pleasant words are like a honeycomb,
sweetness to the soul and health to the bones.
PROVERBS 16:24

Sweet, positive words from you can bring joy and confidence to your child. Children need to hear that they are loved and appreciated. When you speak words of encouragement to your child, you are giving him or her building blocks for life. Let your child know each day he or she is special in your eyes and in the eyes of God.

Everyone needs to know they are loved.

Me

You Are God's Jewel

The Lord says, "As surely as I live, your
children will be like jewels."
ISAIAH 49:18 ICB

You have been created as a special jewel by God. In His eyes, you are more precious than diamonds and rubies. His desire for you is to be the best person possible. That is why He has surrounded you with His love, mercy, and grace. Let each day be filled with His presence and include Him in all that you do.

When you walk with Him,
He will bless you with His favor.

Mommy

The Lord Wants the Best for You

May the LORD give you increase more and more,
you and your children.
May you be blessed by the LORD,
who made heaven and earth.
PSALM 115:14–15

God desires to bless you and your child and give you a life of meaning and purpose. God has placed an intuitive sense of responsibility and need to care for the child you have been given. When you choose to honor Him and include Him in your life, He has promised to bless you with wisdom and understanding.

God wants to bless you.

God Is the Great Provider

God is able to make all grace abound toward you,
that you, always having all sufficiency in all things,
may have an abundance for every good work.
2 Corinthians 9:8

God has blessed you, and His grace will hold you up. Every step you take and every word you speak, God is there encouraging you to be everything He has planned for you to be. God wants an abundant life for you, and His grace will make that possible.

God wants the very best for you.

Mommy

We Are Partners with Christ

For we have become partakers of Christ if we hold
the beginning of our confidence steadfast to the end.
HEBREWS 3:14

It is very important that you share your faith openly
with those in your family. None of us can progress in
our faith without the help and encouragement of fellow
believers in Christ. When the love of Christ is openly
professed in your home, it will spread to everyone in your
family. As a mother, you are one of the pillars that holds
your home together. Hold on to the only One who will
save you and your loved ones—Jesus Christ.

💜💜💜💜

Place your faith firmly in Christ.

Me

We Belong to God

Know that the LORD, He is God;
It is He who has made us, and not we ourselves;
We are His people and the sheep of His pasture.
PSALM 100:3

God is the Shepherd and we are His flock. God is the Creator and we are His creation. God is the Father and we are His children. When you remember these basic truths, life will go a lot smoother. Let each day be filled with His presence.

God wants to take care of you.

Mommy

Bear Fruit

"I am the vine, you are the branches.
He who abides in Me, and I in him, bears much fruit;
for without Me you can do nothing."
John 15:5

When you choose to abide in Christ, spend time with Him, and obey His Word, you will bear much fruit. You were designed by God. This scripture reminds you that without Christ, you can accomplish nothing of permanent, spiritual value. Let each day be filled with His presence, seek Him through prayer, and spend time feeding on His Word. When you do, you will bear much fruit, and God will be glorified.

You can do anything He calls you to do.

Me

Nothing Is Impossible for God

For with God nothing will be impossible.
LUKE 1:37

You have been created in God's image, and through Him all things are possible. As you learn more about God, you will see things through His eyes. What may seem impossible to you is not impossible to God. God desires that you walk closely with Him and be fulfilled in all that you choose to do.

With God, all things are possible.

Mommy

Love One Another

> *"A new commandment I give to you, that you*
> *love one another; as I have loved you, that you*
> *also love one another. By this all will know that you*
> *are My disciples, if you have love for one another."*
> JOHN 13:34–35

The love you display to those around you will be a strong indicator of the person you have become. Jesus commands you to love one another as He has loved you—especially in caring for those in your family. A mother's love is contagious when it is demonstrated every day. If God's loving Spirit is a part of your life, you will be blessed, and so will those around you.

Love others as God loves you.

Me

This Is the Way—Walk in Truth

*I have no greater joy than to hear that
my children walk in truth.*
3 JOHN 4

From the moment you are born until you are an adult, the time you spend developing the way of truth will pay dividends of joy and peace within your heart. When you walk in truth and believe in the Word of God, the power of the Holy Spirit will surround you and bring great joy to you. There is no substitute for knowing the truth about your Creator.

You can share God's joy when you walk in truth.

Mommy

Follow the Shepherd

"My sheep hear My voice, and I know them, and they follow Me. And I give them eternal life, and they shall never perish; neither shall anyone snatch them out of My hand."

JOHN 10:27–28

You belong to Christ, and your eternal life cannot be taken away. The Father holds you by His righteous right hand, and nothing or no one can separate you from the love of Christ. Meditate on these words, teach them to your child, and praise God for His loving mercy and grace. Allow His presence to fill you each day, and look forward expectantly to the leading of His Spirit.

Nothing can separate you from the love of Christ.

Me

The Love for Christ Begins in Your Heart

[I pray] that Christ may dwell in your hearts through
faith; that you, being rooted and grounded in love . . .
may be filled with all the fullness of God.
EPHESIANS 3:17, 19

You are God's child, and He has placed in your heart
a great desire to love Him. Let His love surround
you and fill you each day that you may grow strong in
your faith. Share the wonderful love of God with others.
When you allow His love to be a part of who you are,
His joy will flow through you.

Enjoy a close relationship with God.

Mommy

Let Jesus Come In

> *"Behold, I stand at the door and knock. If anyone hears My voice and opens the door, I will come in to him and dine with him, and he with Me."*
> ### REVELATION 3:20

This is a beautiful picture of Christ knocking on your door, wishing to come into your life to spend time loving, caring for, and enjoying fellowship with you. When you allow Jesus to come into your life, His peace will fill you, and you will be blessed. God desires to be a part of your daily life, where you depend on His wisdom to be the mother you long to be. So spend time alone with your heavenly Father—He wants to hear from you.

Accept God's open invitation.

Me

Eternal Life Is a Gift from God

God has given us eternal life, and this life is in His Son. He who has the Son has life.
1 JOHN 5:11–12

God has promised you eternal life through His Son, Jesus Christ. It is not a wage to be earned, but a gift to be received from God. When you ask the Lord Jesus to come into your heart through faith, He forgives your sins, and gives you an eternal home in heaven. This is a promise that God has given because of His great love for you. He wants very much to welcome you into His family.

God wants you to know Him, love Him, and obey Him.

Mommy

The Lord Is Your Security

For the LORD God is a sun and shield; the LORD
will give grace and glory; no good thing will He
withhold from those who walk uprightly.
PSALM 84:11

When your life is filled with the Lord and you walk with Him, He has promised to be your "sun and shield" to protect you and place good things in your life. Spend each day praising God for His glorious grace. Speak boldly of His love for you, and let your child know just how much the love of God means to you.

Rest in the Lord's protection.

Me

God Protects Those Who Know Him

He shall give His angels charge over you,
To keep you in all your ways.
In their hands they shall bear you up,
Lest you dash your foot against a stone.
PSALM 91:11–12

God provides His angels to watch over you. When you ask for His protection, He will be there. God wants your relationship with Him to be filled with joy and gladness. You are His advertisement to the world of His goodness and mercy. You have been promised God's protection, so do not hesitate to seek God's wisdom and pray daily for Him to help you in everything you do.

God will protect you.

Mommy

Finding Life

For whoever finds me finds life,
and obtains favor from the LORD.
PROVERBS 8:35

God has promised that when you find His wisdom, He will supply everything you need in life. He desires for you to be successful as a person, a mother, and someone who cares deeply about your family and your daily walk with God. Open your heart today and let your loving, heavenly Father fill you with His presence.

God's favor is waiting for you.

Me

You Are God's Gift

"Take heed that you do not despise one of these
little ones, for I say to you that in heaven their angels
always see the face of My Father who is in heaven."
MATTHEW 18:10

In the eyes of God, you are precious. His love for you is unconditional and everlasting. Learn to celebrate every gift that God has given you. You are blessed, and He is watching over you. Let the joy of the Lord fill your heart with love and laughter.

God is watching over you.

Mommy

When You Pray, He Will Answer

*Call to Me, and I will answer you, and show you
great and mighty things, which you do not know.*
JEREMIAH 33:3

The time you spend in prayerful conversation with
God is an essential part of your walk with Christ.
He yearns to hear from you and He will give you all the
answers you need as a mother. He has given you an open
invitation to call to Him anytime, anywhere, and for any
reason. There are many things He wishes to share with
you that will bring joy, peace, and comfort.

God is waiting to hear from you.

Me

Help Is Just a Prayer Away

My help comes from the LORD.
PSALM 121:2

God never intended for you to go through life alone. He is with you in all that you will do. His peace will surround you in times of chaos and joy and in each experience you encounter. Let God be your Helper. Let Him embrace you and be your Blessing-Giver.

God's wisdom is there for the asking.

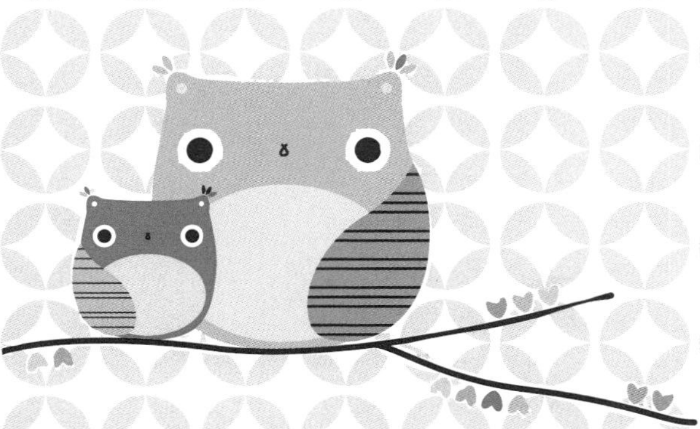